CITIES OF NORTH AMERICA

ROB HUNT

ILLUSTRATED BY VICTOR BEUREN

W
FRANKLIN WATTS
LONDON • SYDNEY

Franklin Watts
First published in Great Britain in 2021
by The Watts Publishing Group

Copyright © The Watts Publishing Group 2021

All rights reserved

Credits
Artwork by Victor Beuren
Design: Collaborate Agency
Editor: Nicola Edwards

ISBN 978 1 4451 6893 7 (hb); 978 1 4451 6894 4 (pb)

Printed in Dubai

Franklin Watts
An imprint of
Hachette Children's Group
Part of the Watts Publishing Group
Carmelite House
50 Victoria Embankment
London EC4Y 0DZ

An Hachette UK Company
www.hachette.co.uk

www.hachettechildrens.co.uk

FSC
MIX
Paper from responsible sources
FSC® C104740

CONTENTS

Cities of North America — 4

Mexico City, Mexico — 6

Toronto, Canada — 10

New York, USA — 14

Havana, Cuba — 18

Montreal, Canada — 22

Nuuk, Greenland — 26

Washington, D.C, USA — 30

Managua, Nicaragua — 34

San Francisco, USA — 38

Guatemala City, Guatemala — 42

More North American Cities — 46

   Ottawa, Canada

   San Juan, Puerto Rico

   Kingston, Jamaica

   Calgary, Canada

   Las Vegas, USA

   Chicago, USA

   Port-au-Prince, Haiti

   Tegucigalpa, Honduras

Glossary and index — 48

CITIES OF NORTH AMERICA

Welcome to North America, the world's third-largest continent by area, after Asia and Africa. It contains 23 sovereign states and some of the most exciting cities on the planet!

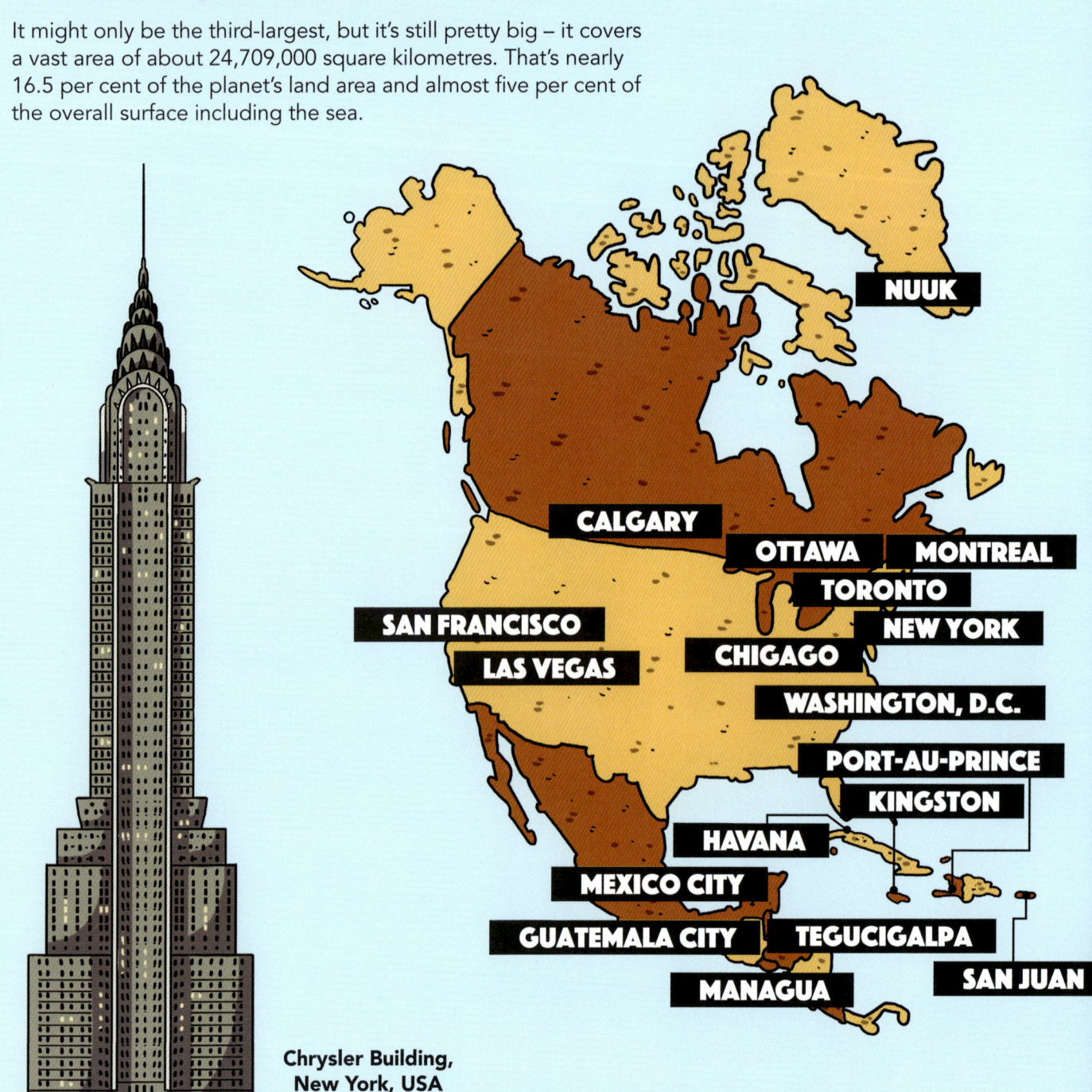

It might only be the third-largest, but it's still pretty big – it covers a vast area of about 24,709,000 square kilometres. That's nearly 16.5 per cent of the planet's land area and almost five per cent of the overall surface including the sea.

NUUK
CALGARY
OTTAWA
MONTREAL
TORONTO
SAN FRANCISCO
NEW YORK
LAS VEGAS
CHIGAGO
WASHINGTON, D.C.
PORT-AU-PRINCE
KINGSTON
HAVANA
MEXICO CITY
GUATEMALA CITY
TEGUCIGALPA
SAN JUAN
MANAGUA

Chrysler Building, New York, USA

North America has extremes in height and in temperature. Its highest point is Denali in Alaska at 6,194 metres and its lowest is Death Valley in California, which is 86 m below sea level. Death Valley is also among the hottest places on Earth, with temperatures reaching 56.7°C! The coldest North American city is Iqaluit in Canada. It has recorded a temperature of −45.6°C, which makes it one of the coldest cities in the world.

North America is home to 596 million people, about 8 percent of the world's population. It is a figure that has grown very rapidly – when the Europeans, led by Christopher Columbus, first arrived in 1492, populations of around 50 million had been living in North and South America for around 15,000 years.

The two continents, together, were then known as 'The New World'. That's because, at that time, their landmass was largely unknown to the 'Old World' of Africa, Asia and Europe. Their 'discovery' brought untold riches to 'The Old World', but was devastating to the Indigenous people of the Americas. The subsequent years that led to the growth of the cities in this book were prosperous for many but others suffered disease, slavery, displacement, injustice and death.

Denali, Alaska, USA

The people and the cities that survived became some of the most prosperous nations ever to have existed. North America is now, arguably, the most powerful continent on the planet.

The amazing cities in this book have developed in a relatively short time. They've suffered hardship and many setbacks along the way, but the people of these cities have created and achieved many great things, including putting the first human on the Moon.

So dig out your passport and get ready to explore the cities of North America!

The tallest building in CDMX is the **246.6-m Torre Reforma**. It has strange window patterns that have led some people to nickname it the 'Tetris Building' after the famous tile-stacking game.

Built in 1997, the **Calakmul building** is in the business area of CDMX. It's known by the locals as 'La Lavadora' (the washing machine) and with its huge, circle cut-outs it is easy to see why. The triangular-shaped building next door is part of the same Calakmul complex.

The name **Calakmul** comes from an ancient Mayan site and means 'city of the two pyramids'.

Anyone lucky enough to attend the **University City of Mexico** (Ciudad Universitaria) will study in some of the most beautiful educational buildings in the world. Many of them are decorated with wonderful murals by David Alfaro Siqueiros and Juan O'Gorman. O'Gorman's mural at the central library is made from millions of coloured stones collected from around Mexico.

MEXICO CITY
MEXICO

'Hola y bienvenido a' ('hello and welcome to') Mexico City, the capital city of – you guessed it – Mexico! It's proper Spanish title is Ciudad de México (City of Mexico) and it's often shortened to just CDMX. With a population of around 21 million it is the largest Spanish-speaking city on the planet and the biggest city in North America.

The campus also includes the **Estadio Olímpico Universitario**, built in 1952 and used for the 1968 Olympic Games. The whole university campus was made a UNESCO World Heritage Site in 2007.

Arcos Bosques is an office building and a shopping complex. It consists of two towers. **Tower I** is nicknamed 'The Trousers' and is two towers joined at the top by a section called a lintel. It has its own helipad on the roof.

Tower II is also two columns but this time joined in the mid-section.

HISTORY

The history of Mexico City begins with the founding of the Aztec city Mēxihco-Tenōchtitlan around 1325 by the Mexica people, making it the oldest city in this book! It was built on an island in Lake Texcoco and often became flooded.

When the Spanish invaded the area in the sixteenth century they spotted its strategic importance, conquered it and began to build the city that stands there today. The lake was drained in the seventeenth century to prevent flooding. While flooding is no longer a problem, earthquakes certainly are. The 1985 earthquake killed 10,000 people in Mexico City. Buildings there have to be very well constructed to cope with the frequent tremors.

MONEY

The Mexican peso is the currency of Mexico. The name comes from the Spanish for weight. The terms originally used were *peso ora* (gold weight) and *peso plata* (silver weight).

PLACES TO GO

Frida Kahlo House
Mexico City has a rich cultural heritage and has been home to many famous artists. One of the best-known is Frida Kahlo. You can visit the distinctive blue house that she shared with her artist husband Diego Rivera as it has been turned into a museum dedicated to her life and work.

Museo Soumaya
For a wider range of Mexican art you will need to visit the **Museo Soumaya**. It has Mexican art dating from 3,000 years ago to the present. It also has a fabulous collection of works by European artists including Rodin, Dalí, da Vinci, Van Gogh and Renoir.

Frida Kahlo Museum

MEXICO CITY
MEXICO

FOOD

Churros and chocolate

Mexican food is famous around the world. The place to sample some of the best is on a walk through the downtown area. Churros, which are deep-fried pastries, are often dipped in chocolate and are great for snacking on at any time of day.

Tortillas, tostadas and much more

In ancient times the Mayans would wrap fish in corn tortillas and fish tacos are still a popular Mexican dish. In fact, all the Mexican favourites can be enjoyed here. Tacos, enchiladas, tamales and tostadas are famous the world over for a reason – they are adaptable (you can have them with any meat or vegetables) and they are very tasty!

If you are feeling a little more adventurous you might care to tuck in to some escamoles, or pan-fried ant larvae. They were prized as a delicacy by the Aztecs and taste like nutty cottage cheese ... yum!

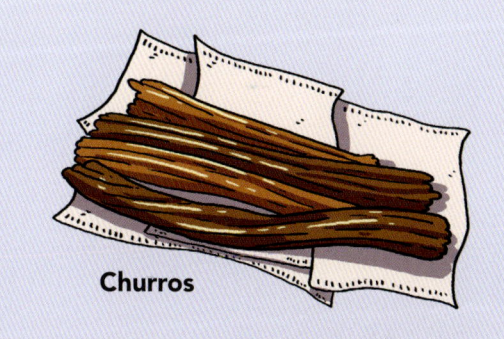

Churros

Pan-fried ant larvae

Cathedral of Art

National Palace

THINGS TO DO

See the ancient city centre
The site at the centre of the ancient city is now the Zócalo, a large square that is bordered by the **Metropolitan Cathedral** to the north, and the **National Palace** to the east.

Visit the 'Cathedral of Art'
A short walk from the Zócalo, is the **Palacio de Bellas Artes**, where you can experience ballet, opera, theatre and other arts in a fabulous building nicknamed the 'Cathedral of Art in Mexico'.

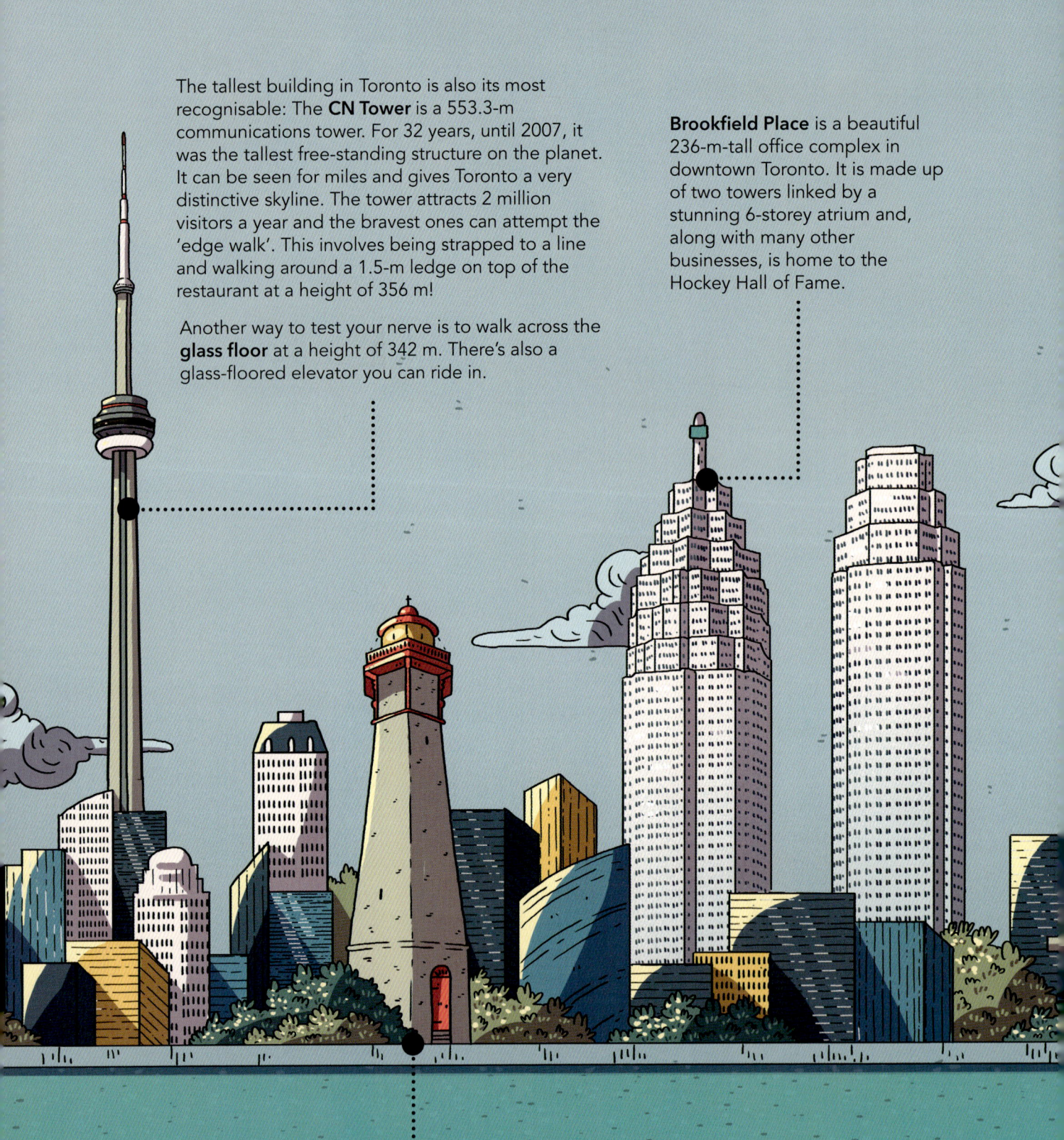

The tallest building in Toronto is also its most recognisable: The **CN Tower** is a 553.3-m communications tower. For 32 years, until 2007, it was the tallest free-standing structure on the planet. It can be seen for miles and gives Toronto a very distinctive skyline. The tower attracts 2 million visitors a year and the bravest ones can attempt the 'edge walk'. This involves being strapped to a line and walking around a 1.5-m ledge on top of the restaurant at a height of 356 m!

Another way to test your nerve is to walk across the **glass floor** at a height of 342 m. There's also a glass-floored elevator you can ride in.

Brookfield Place is a beautiful 236-m-tall office complex in downtown Toronto. It is made up of two towers linked by a stunning 6-storey atrium and, along with many other businesses, is home to the Hockey Hall of Fame.

The **Gibraltar Point Lighthouse** is one of the oldest buildings in the city. It was built in 1808 and some say that it has its very own ghost – the spirit of the first lighthouse keeper, who was murdered. It is located on the largest of a small group of islands that lie a short distance from Toronto on Lake Huron.

TORONTO
CANADA

How's it going, eh? You've arrived in Toronto, the capital of the Canadian province of Ontario and the most populated city in Canada. Nearly 3 million people live in the city and nearly 6 million live in the larger Toronto metropolitan area. It's situated on Lake Huron, the second-largest of the Great Lakes.

Opened in 1965, **Toronto City Hall** is one of the most distinctive buildings in the city. It is in Nathan Phillips Square, which lights up spectacularly at night with a huge 3D sign spelling out the name of the city. The square also has a reflecting pool and a skating rink, so offers a wonderful photo opportunity.

Perhaps the most unusual building in town is the **Sharp Centre for Design**, which is attached to the main building of the Ontario College of Art and Design University. It is a curious black and white box supported by a series of irregular multicoloured pillars and is nicknamed the 'shoebox in the sky' or 'the tabletop'.

HISTORY

The word Toronto means either a narrow channel of water, or 'a place where trees stand in water' in the Mohawk language. In the seventeenth century it was used to describe the area at the mouth of the Humber River. The City of Toronto eventually took the name in 1834. Previously it had been called York and there are still several districts in the city with 'York' in their name, such as East York and North York.

MONEY

The local currency is the Canadian dollar. The one-dollar coin depicts a Canadian water bird called a loon and because of this most Canadians call the coin a 'loonie'. The two-dollar coin is known as a 'toonie'.

THINGS TO DO

Watch an ice hockey match

The number one sport in Canada is ice hockey, so make sure you go and see the Toronto Maple Leafs play at the Scotiabank Arena. It's not for the nervous though – expect a full-on contact sport with plenty of clashes and sometimes even blood on the ice!

Visit a secretive castle

A Canadian castle is a rare thing to behold. Although it looks old, Casa Loma was actually completed in 1914. It took three years to build and has 98 rooms, as well as towers, fountains and secret tunnels!

Casa Loma

TORONTO
CANADA

FOOD

Maple syrup heaven

Canada's most famous food export is maple syrup. It is made from the sap of maple trees. Genuine Canadian maple syrup must be made entirely from sap and not mixed with any other sugars. It is used to sweeten foods and poured on breakfast dishes, such as pancakes and bacon. In winter you can try 'taffy on the snow' – maple syrup is heated, poured on snow and then rolled around a stick.

Butter tarts

Butter tarts are another famous Canadian dessert. They are so well-loved that Canadians hold competitions to see who can make the best ones. They are made with butter, sugar, syrup and egg, and baked in a pastry shell until the inside is semi-solid with a crispy top.

Maple syrup pancakes

Butter tart

PLACES TO GO

Royal Ontario Museum

History and art lovers can visit one of Toronto's more dramatic buildings: the Royal Ontario Museum. The exterior looks like a spaceship has crashed into an old building!

The museum houses a selection of natural history exhibits, including many dinosaurs, and galleries devoted to world art and culture from the Iron Age to the present day.

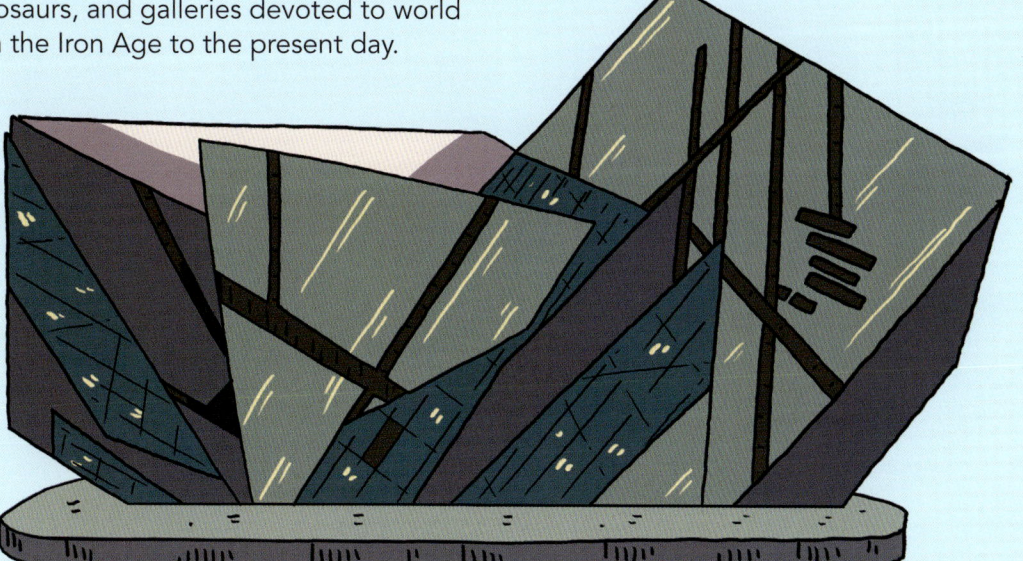

Royal Ontario Museum

13

The island borough of Manhattan has probably the most famous skyline in the world and has the second-highest number of skyscrapers after Hong Kong. It is connected to the other boroughs by ferry boats, tunnels and bridges. The most famous bridge is probably the **Brooklyn Bridge**, built in 1883.

At 541 m, the tallest building in New York is the **One World Trade Center**. It stands near the site of the twin towers of the original World Trade Center. Those towers were destroyed on September 11th, 2001 in a terrorist attack. The current building stands as a memorial to those who died, but also functions as an office building. 541 m is 1776 feet in imperial measures. This figure was chosen because 1776 was the year in which the United States declared independence from Great Britain.

One of the most beautiful buildings in Manhattan is the Art Deco **Chrysler Building.** It was completed in 1930 and, at 318.9 m, was the world's tallest building for 11 months.

NEW YORK
USA

'Yo!', 'Ciao!' or 'Hola!' from New York, one of the most cosmopolitan cities on the planet. The locals call it 'The Big Apple', but nobody really seems to know why. The city has a population of around 8.2 million living in five famous boroughs: the Bronx, Brooklyn, Manhattan, Queens and Staten Island.

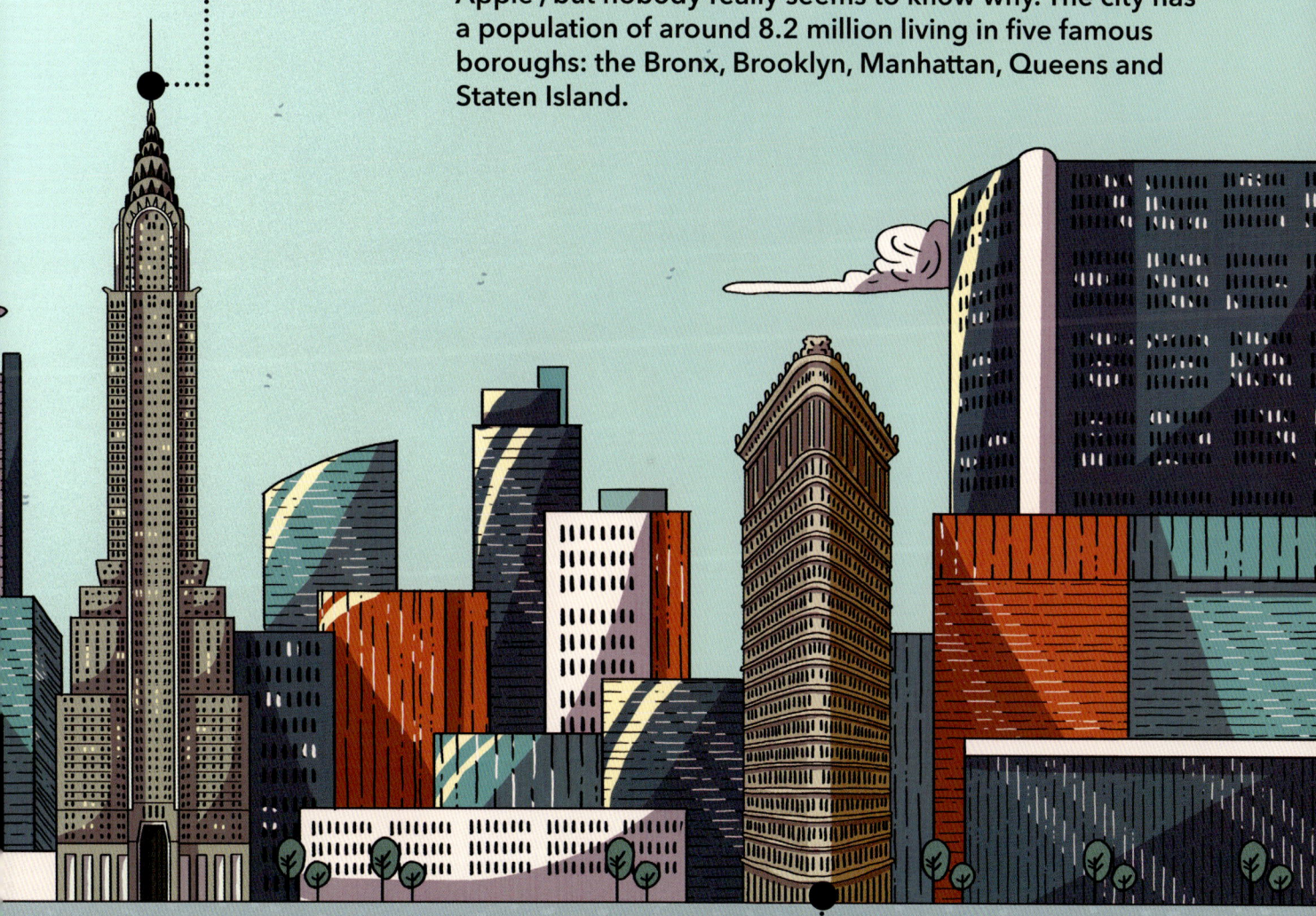

The **Empire State Building** became the highest building in the world in April 1931. It measures 443 m to its tip. Two years later, the film *King Kong* featured a giant gorilla climbing to the top of the building to fight aeroplanes. The building instantly became world-famous.

One of the earliest 'skyscrapers' was the **Fuller Building**, which opened in 1902. Its unusual, triangular shape earned it the name the **Flatiron Building**. At 86.9 m and only 21 floors high, it wouldn't be classed as a skyscraper today, but it was one of the tallest buildings of its time and remains one of the city's most distinctive buildings.

HISTORY

When the British captured New Amsterdam from the Dutch, they renamed it New York (after the Duke of York, rather than the City of York). Between 1785 and 1790, after the American War of Independence, New York was briefly the capital of the USA. Since 1886, the millions of immigrants arriving in the city have been greeted by the Statue of Liberty. The copper statue was a gift from France.

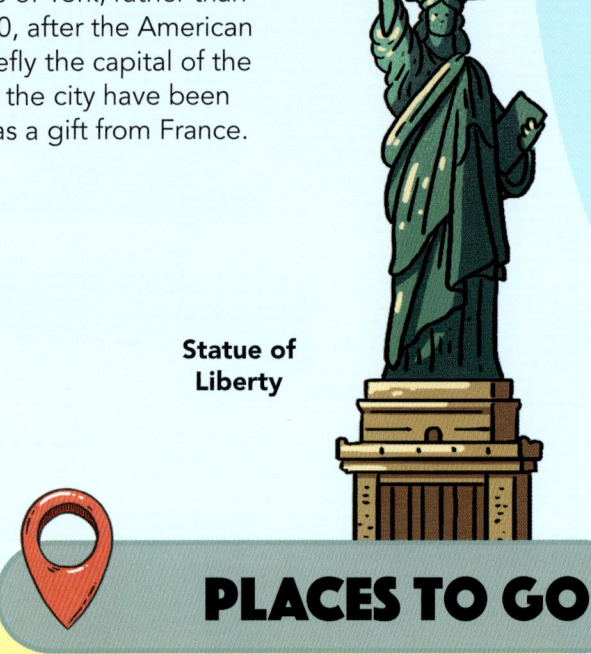

MONEY

New York's Wall Street is one of the biggest financial centres in the world. Its Stock Exchange is internationally famous and the most important currency in the world is the US dollar.

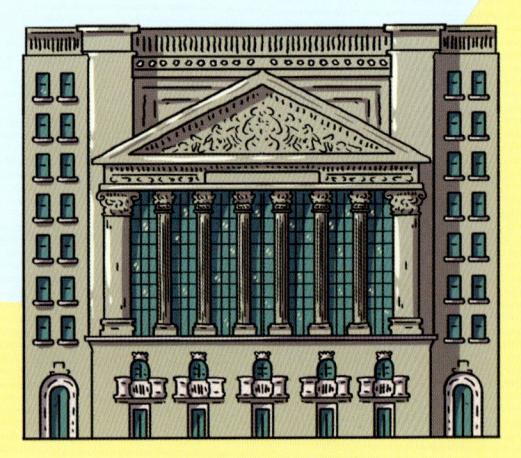

Statue of Liberty

PLACES TO GO

The Guggenheim

The Solomon R. Guggenheim Museum not only houses works of art, it is itself a work of art. It was designed by Frank Lloyd Wright and opened in 1959. It was originally called 'The Museum of Non-Objective Painting' and it has a huge collection of modern art. If you think the outside looks impressive, wait until you see the huge spiral ramp on the inside!

The New York Stock Exchange

The Guggenheim

FOOD

NEW YORK
USA

New York is a city of immigrants and those immigrants have all contributed to the culinary melting pot. It would probably be easier to list the foods that you CAN'T get in New York, rather than attempt to list all cuisines on offer, which range from Armenian to Zimbabwean.

One thing you must sample, however, is a New York pizza. The USA's first pizza parlour, Lombardi's, opened in 1905. Be prepared though, do not even try to eat it with a knife and fork! It's fingers only in NYC.

Lombardi's

Pizza

Yellow taxi

THINGS TO DO

Catch a cab

New York is the home of the big yellow taxi. You won't have much trouble seeing or hearing these cars. They are everywhere and many of the drivers like to honk their horns!

Walk the High Line

A 2.33-km walk along the High Line is a great way to spend an afternoon and see some of the sights of east Manhattan. In 2009 the High Line was transformed from an elevated railway line to a beautiful walkway. It's incredibly popular with locals and visitors, offering great views of the Hudson River to one side and the Manhattan skyline to the other.

The High Line

The **Bacardi Building**, opened in 1930, is a beautiful Art Deco construction that originally housed the Bacardi Rum company. It still has the company's bat logo perched on top, but now it is used as offices for a variety of companies.

The **FOCSA Building** is the tallest building in the whole of Cuba. It is 121 m tall and was completed in 1956. There is a restaurant at the top so you can enjoy the views of Havana as you eat. The building also contains apartments, shops, a theatre and TV studios.

El Capitolio, or the National Capitol Building, is one of the most visited sites in Havana. Inside you will find the 30-tonne, 14.6-m, gold-plated bronze Statue of the Republic, a personification of Cuba as a female warrior.

HAVANA
CUBA

'Bienvenido a la Habana!' You have arrived in Havana – the capital city of the Republic of Cuba and home to just over 2 million people. A historical combination of Spanish invasion, African slavery and a struggle with interference from the USA has produced a determined city with a rich culture, and a wide variety of architecture, food and music. It is impossible to be bored in Havana!

Revolution Square commemorates the 1959 revolution and was the location for many of Fidel Castro's long speeches. A trip to the top of the 109-m **José Martí Memorial** will give you great views of the other government buildings nearby, such as the **Palace of the Revolution**, Castro's official office.

The **Russian Embassy** stands out against the Havana skyline because of its startling design. Some people think it looks like a sword, but others see a giant syringe!

The **National Art Schools** were built by Fidel Castro, who led the country after the 1959 revolution. They are considered to be some of the most beautiful buildings in Cuba.

HISTORY

Havana was founded by the Spanish in 1519 and thrived as the largest natural port in the Caribbean. It became so wealthy that it drew the attention of the real pirates of the Caribbean and was attacked and plundered many times. Morro Castle was built in 1589 to give the port protection but Havana was still captured by the British in 1762. Cuba was handed back to the Spanish a year later, and finally gained independence in 1902. From 1953 to 1959 Fidel Castro led a revolution and implemented a socialist system that has governed the country ever since.

Morro Castle

MONEY

The Cuban monetary system can be very confusing! For a start, it has two currencies - many of the locals use the Cuban peso (known as CUP), while visitors use the Cuban convertible peso (CUC). It's very important not to get them mixed up as the CUC is worth a lot more than the CUP! Almost everything you buy as a tourist will be in CUC, but it's worth having a few CUPs for street food or public transport.

Castillo de le Real Fuerza

PLACES TO GO

Old Havana

Make sure to explore La Habana Vieja – Old Havana. It has hundreds of beautiful old buildings from throughout Havana's 500-year history.

The old fort

Completed in 1577, the Castillo de la Real Fuerza is one of the oldest forts in the region and was an early, unsuccessful attempt to defend Havana from pirates.

Museum of the Revolution

The beautiful Museum of the Revolution has a tank outside. This was the one used by Fidel Castro when Cuba resisted the 1961 attempt by the USA to overthrow their government in what became known as 'The Bay of Pigs invasion'.

Museum of the Revolution

HAVANA
CUBA

FOOD

Quimbombo

As you'd expect from a city with such a diverse cultural background, Havana has a lot of different food on offer. The dish with the best name is surely the quimbombo – a stew made with pork, okra and plantain.

Tostones

Plantain is very popular hereso you may care to sample some tostones – fried plantain served with a dip. You can get these at some of the street stalls in Old Havana.

Quimbombo

Tostones

THINGS TO DO

Stroll down the Malecón

Take a walk down the Malecón, an 8-km-long esplanade, for great views of the bay on one side and great views of the classic motorcars speeding past on the other.

View vintage cars

Havana is full of vintage American cars. They were imported until the 1959 revolution, when imports and exports were banned. Cubanos have been making do ever since and keeping the old cars on the road.

Ride in an almendrón

Newer cars from China are starting to replace the ones that can't be repaired. You can ride in an almendrón, a 1950s car that operates as a fixed taxi service between neighbourhoods.

Malecón

Vintage car

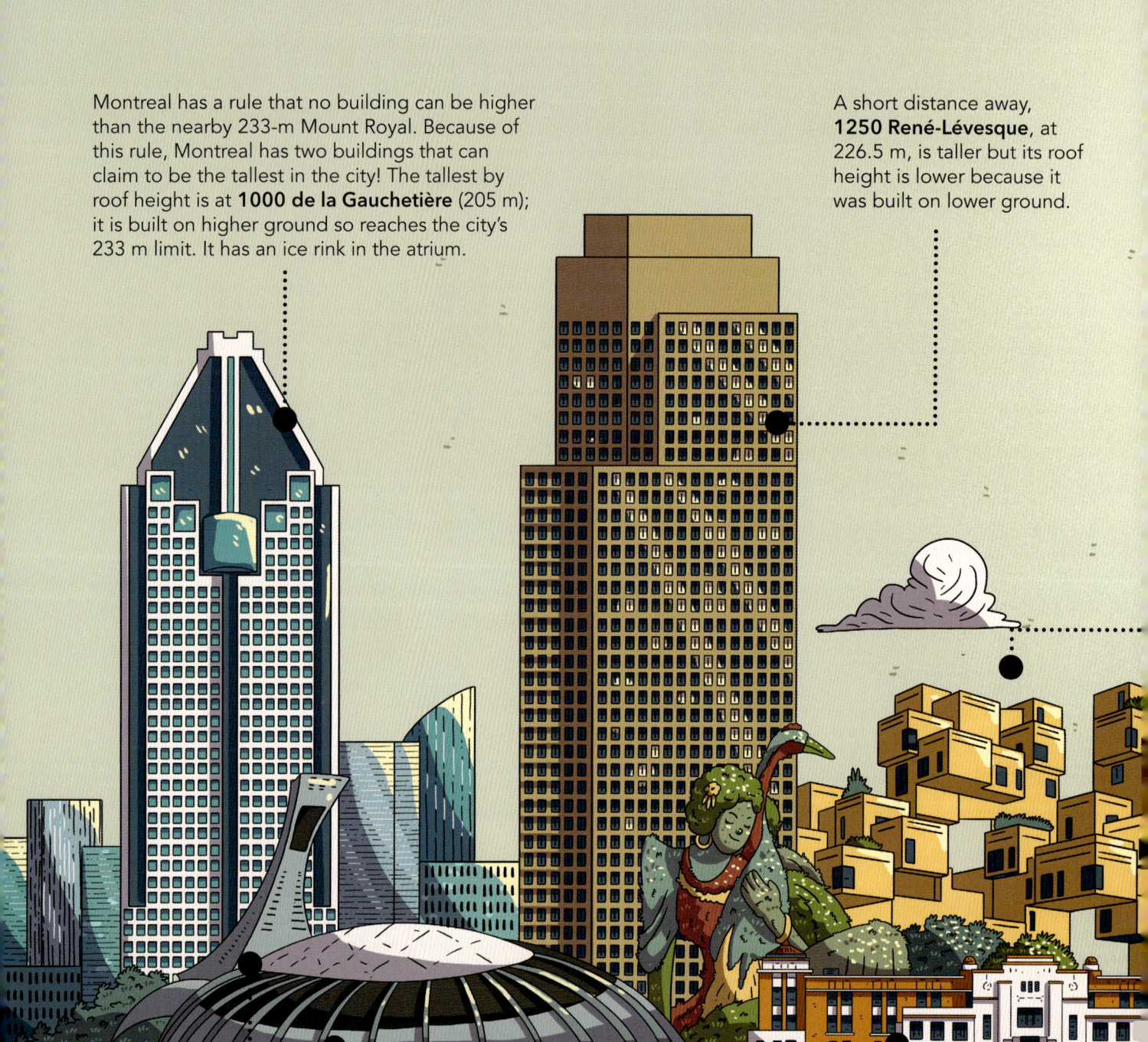

Montreal has a rule that no building can be higher than the nearby 233-m Mount Royal. Because of this rule, Montreal has two buildings that can claim to be the tallest in the city! The tallest by roof height is at **1000 de la Gauchetière** (205 m); it is built on higher ground so reaches the city's 233 m limit. It has an ice rink in the atrium.

A short distance away, **1250 René-Lévesque**, at 226.5 m, is taller but its roof height is lower because it was built on lower ground.

Enjoy the view of the city, including its skyscrapers, the Saint Lawrence River and Mount Royal, from the 175-m-tall **Montreal Tower**, which is attached to the **Olympic Stadium**. It is the tallest tilted tower in the world and you can take a cable car to the top. The stadium was built for the 1976 Olympics, but now hosts other sports matches, exhibitions and music concerts.

The **Montreal Botanical Garden** is an extensive collection of greenhouses and themed gardens near to the Olympic Park. There are Japanese, Chinese, Alpine and First Nation gardens, showing off elements of each of these cultures and environments. It has a beautiful Art Deco pavilion building.

22

MONTREAL
CANADA

'Bonjour!' You've made it to Montreal, the largest city of the Canadian province of Quebec. 1.8 million people make their home in the central city zone and 4.2 million in the wider urban area making it, by population, the second-largest city in the country, after Toronto. French is the official language of Quebec but most people speak English as well. It is the second-largest French-speaking city in the world, after Paris.

In the distance to the east of the skyscrapers is **Habitat 67**, a spectacular housing development built in 1967.

Nearby and in the shadow of the two competing skyscrapers is the **Mary, Queen of the World Cathedral**. It looks like a very old European cathedral but was built in 1894.

Another great old-looking building is **Saint Joseph's Oratory.** This one wasn't completed until 1967! Inside you'll find hundreds of crutches left by people who claim they've been cured by the miraculous powers of the church. The miracles are attributed to Brother André, who built the first chapel on the site and was later made a saint. His heart is kept in a special box in the Oratory.

23

HISTORY

Montreal is named after the nearby mountain – it is French for Mount Royal. It was colonised by the French in the seventeenth century and originally called Ville-Marie (the City of Mary). It is situated on the Island of Montreal in the St Lawrence River and the name of the city was eventually changed to match that of the island. The city was a French settlement, known for its beaver fur trade, until it was conquered by the British in 1760.

MONEY

As Canada was part of the British Empire until 1858, the currency was the Canadian pound. After that it was changed to the Canadian dollar to make trade with the USA easier. As Canada is still a constitutional monarchy, some of the notes still show the British monarch. English speakers call the coin a 'loonie', because of the image of a loon bird on the back. French speakers use the same nickname but in translation, calling the 'loonie' a 'huard'.

PLACES TO GO

Old Montreal

Old Montreal is a great place to spend some time. It is a well-preserved area that has buildings dating from the seventeenth century. You can find out about the city's history at Pointe-à-Callière: Montreal's Museum of Archaeology and History, which stands on the spot where the city was founded in 1642.

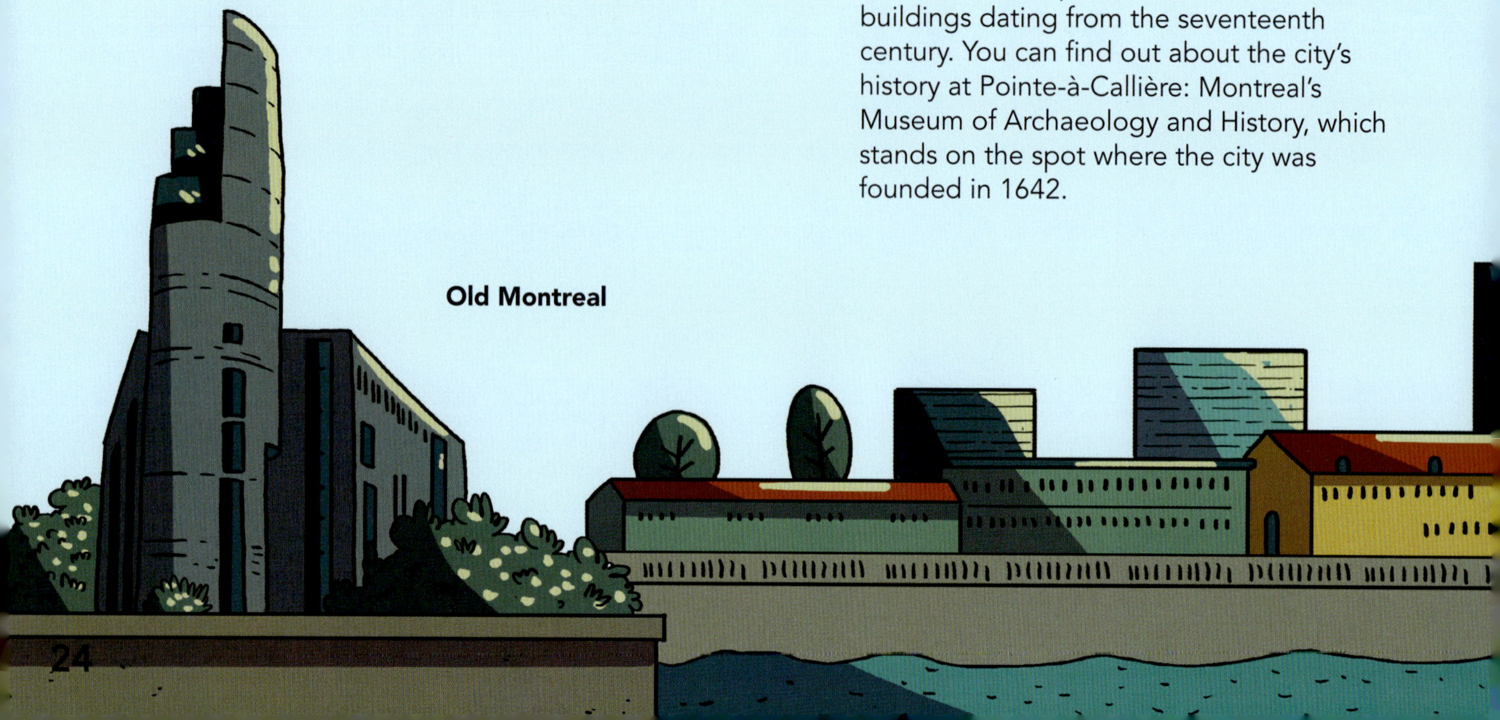

Old Montreal

MONTREAL
CANADA

FOOD

Sweet bagel

The Montreal bagel is smaller, thinner, and denser than an ordinary bagel. It is also much sweeter because the dough is made with honey and eggs. In some stores you can watch Montreal bagels being cooked in wood-fired ovens.

Poutine

Another delicacy to try is poutine – French fries covered in cheese curds and gravy. The Quebecois are very proud of their poutine and some get annoyed when people refer to it as a 'Canada's national dish'. It is Quebecois, they insist, not Canadian!

Sweet Bagels

Poutine

THINGS TO DO

Climb the Clock Tower

The Old Port of Montreal dates from 1611 when it was the centre of the fur trade. It has a famous 45-m-tall clock tower and if you can manage the 192 steps to the top you'll have a great view over the city.

Clock Tower

Spend a day at Saint Helen's Island

Saint Helen's Island is in the middle of the Saint Lawrence River. It has the Aquatic Complex and La Ronde amusement park. The great biosphere was completed in 1967 and today it houses a museum with environmental exhibits.

The tallest building in the whole of Greenland is the **Nuuk Center**, a shopping mall. It is only 10 stories high, but it should give you the best view of the city and Sermitsiaq (Saddle Mountain) a distinctive 1,210-m peak, which can be seen from just about anywhere in the city.

The oldest building in Greenland is **Hans Egede House**, which was built in 1728. Hans was a Danish missionary who introduced Christianity to the native Inuit people. He also wrote a report of seeing a sea monster while sailing off the Greenland coast. He described it as a 'terrible creature' taller than the ship's mast, with a small head and large fins.

The **Katuaq cultural centre** is a modern building, opened in 1997, that is used for concerts and exhibitions in Nuuk. The wavy design is inspired by the movements of the Aurora Borealis (Northern Lights) and the dramatic scenery of the Arctic.

Another modern building is the **University of Greenland** – the only university in the country. It was founded in 1987 and moved into this interestingly shapped building, known as Llimmaefik in 2009.

NUUK
GREENLAND

The University of Greenland had previously been housed in the **Moravian Brethren Mission House**, which dates from 1747.

'Aluu' ('Hello') from Nuuk, the capital city of Greenland, where many of the 18,000 population speak Greenlandic, an Inuit language. Although Greenland is on the North American continent, it is governed by Denmark, and not classed as a country on its own – it's an autonomous territory. This means that Nuuk is actually a European city! It is also the most northern capital on the planet, just a few kilometres further north than Rekjavik, the northernmost capital of a country: Iceland.

Nuuk is famous for its **colourful houses**. Originally the buildings' different colours indicated what they were used for: houses connected to trade or religion were red; hospitals were yellow; police stations were black; the telephone company was green; and factories were blue. Orange, pink and purple houses have since been added and people can paint them whatever colour they like.

The most popular sport in the country is handball. You can watch matches at the **Inuvik indoor arena**. It is next to Nuuk Stadium which, unsurprisingly given the climate, has an all-weather artificial pitch. The stadium hosts football matches and music concerts.

27

HISTORY

After European settlement, the city was established as a Norwegian colony called Godthåb (Good Hope in Danish) in 1728. The area had been inhabited by Indigenous people since 2200 BCE. The Norwegian settlers were missionaries trying to bring Christianity to the Inuits. The city adopted the Greenlandic name 'Nuuk' in 1979. It means 'Cape' – the type of coastal landform that the city sits upon. About a third of Greenland's entire population live here.

MONEY

Because it is governed by Denmark, Greenland uses the Danish krone as its currency.

PLACES TO GO

Nuuk Art Museum

The permanent exhibition at Nuuk Art Museum has a lot of historical art by artists connected to Greenland. The dramatic Arctic landscape and the lives of the Inuit are represented in many of the paintings. There are regular exhibitions of modern art.

Niels Lynge's House

Nearby is Niels Lynge's House. He was an artist who built and decorated his house in the 1950s. It is preserved in the style of the era with Niels' paintings on display.

The Greenland National Museum

A visit to the Greenland National Museum is not for the faint-hearted. One of the main exhibits is of some mummified bodies found in the north of the country. The bodies date from 1475 and are incredibly well preserved because they were freeze-dried by the harsh weather.

Nuuk Art Museum

Niels Lynge's House

The Greenland National Museum

FOOD

NUUK
GREENLAND

Raw whale

In Nuuk you can find out what whales taste like – if you want to! Whale meat is an important part of Nuuk cuisine. Muktuk is a dish of raw whale skin and blubber, which is a good source of vitamin C.

Seal soup

The country's national dish is a soup called 'suaasat'. It is traditionally made from seal, but sometimes it contains whale, reindeer or even seabirds. If you have a spare seagull, and want to make your own, the other ingredients are onions, potatoes, salt and pepper. Enjoy!

Muktuk

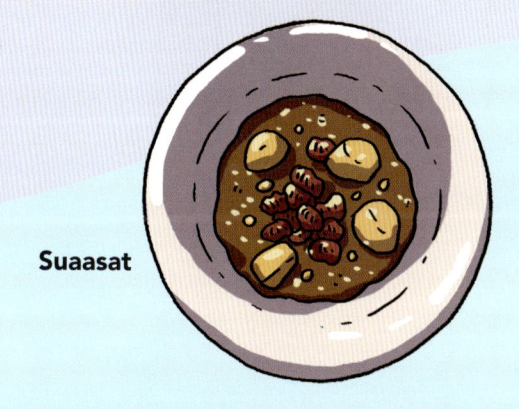

Suaasat

THINGS TO DO

The Northern Lights

See the Northern Lights

If you're in Nuuk in autumn or winter time you may get to see the incredible Aurora Borealis, also known as the Northern Lights. The light show is caused by electrically charged particles from the Sun hitting gases in the Earth's atmosphere and releasing light energy.

Whale watch

If you visit in the summer, that is the best time to go whale watching. If you are really lucky you may spot the long tusk of a narwhal poking through the water.

Narwhal

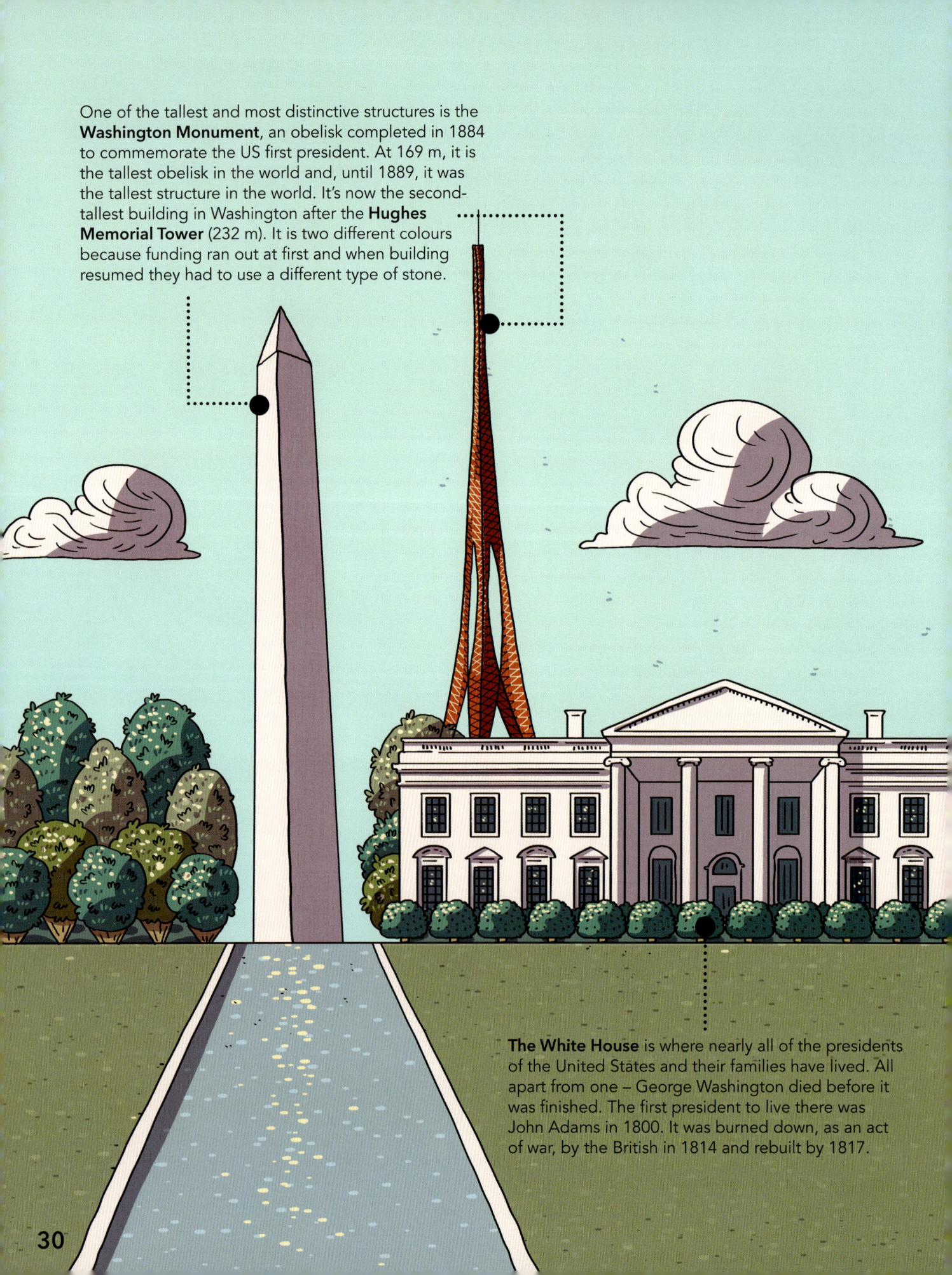

One of the tallest and most distinctive structures is the **Washington Monument**, an obelisk completed in 1884 to commemorate the US first president. At 169 m, it is the tallest obelisk in the world and, until 1889, it was the tallest structure in the world. It's now the second-tallest building in Washington after the **Hughes Memorial Tower** (232 m). It is two different colours because funding ran out at first and when building resumed they had to use a different type of stone.

The White House is where nearly all of the presidents of the United States and their families have lived. All apart from one – George Washington died before it was finished. The first president to live there was John Adams in 1800. It was burned down, as an act of war, by the British in 1814 and rebuilt by 1817.

WASHINGTON, D.C.
USA

'Hi!' You've arrived in Washington, D.C., the capital city of the United States. D.C. stands for the District of Columbia and the city is known as D.C. to its population of around 700,000. The city is the site for many iconic buildings and a lot of them are in walking distance of each other. Compared to other U.S. cities, D.C. is quite low-rise because it has a 140-foot (about 40 metres – the USA uses imperial measures) limit on how tall buildings can be.

The capital city is where the government of a country sits, but a capitol building is where the elected politicians make the laws. The **Capitol Building** in Washington, D.C. was designed and built at the end of the eighteenth century, after a British doctor and amateur architect, William Thornton, won a competition set by the Secretary of State at the time, Thomas Jefferson. His prize was 500 dollars.

Thornton went on to design the **Octagon House** in the wonderfully named area of Foggy Bottom. It's now a museum and has a reputation as the most haunted house in D.C.. The ghosts of slaves are said to ring bells to announce their presence.

HISTORY

Founded in 1790, Washington, D.C. was designed to be the capital city of the newly formed United States of America and not attached to any existing state. The USA was sometimes called Columbia (a feminised version of Columbus – the first European to explore the continent) in those days, so the seat of government was called The District of Columbia. All of the states of the Union have a street in D.C. named after them. The White House is number 1600 on Pennsylvania Avenue, often nicknamed 'America's Main Street'.

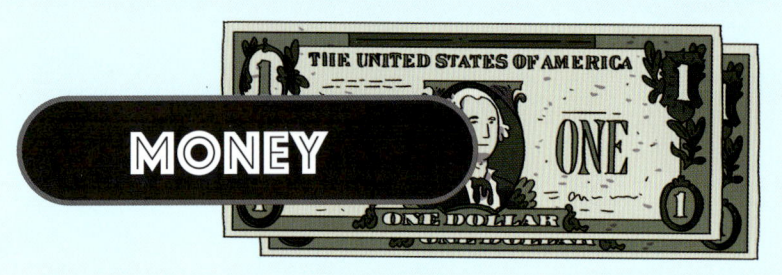

MONEY

The local currency is the US dollar. In Washington, your wallet can act as a tour guide! The one-dollar bill (or note) has a picture of the first president, who gave his name to the capital.

The five-dollar bill has the Lincoln Memorial on it; the 10-dollar bill shows the Treasury Building; the 20-dollar one has the White House on it; and if you're lucky enough to have a fifty-dollar bill, it shows the Capitol Building.

PLACES TO GO

The National Museum of the American Indian

If you enjoy modern architecture you may like to visit the National Museum of the American Indian. This museum is dedicated to telling the story of the Indigenous people of America and how their lives were drastically altered by the arrival of the Europeans.

The National Museum of the American Indian

WASHINGTON, D.C.
USA

FOOD

Chili sausage

D.C.'s signature dish is the 'half-smoke'. It's a spicy dish of half-beef, half-pork smoked sausage covered in chili. You can find them anywhere, but the most famous ones are from Ben's Chili Bowl, which has served them up to President Obama and many other celebrities.

Ben's Chili Bowl

The National Cathedral

Ford's Theatre

THINGS TO DO

See if you can spot Darth Vader

The National Cathedral has lots of gargoyles and grotesques. If you look carefully you might be able to spot Darth Vader! He's there because children were asked to send in designs when the north-west tower was built in the 1980s.

Visit the scene of a crime

If you want to see a play, and catch a slice of history at the same time, then you should visit Ford's Theatre. This is the site where President Abraham Lincoln was shot in 1865. It is still a theatre and shows plays but it also has a museum devoted to the assassination.

Over the years, devastating earthquakes, hurricanes and civil war have wrought great damage on Managua. Partly because of this, it is a low-rise city with no skyscrapers and very few old buildings: it's too risky to build skyscrapers, and old buildings keep getting destroyed! Nevertheless it has a lot of interesting architecture.

Probably the most famous building is known as the **Old Cathedral of Managua** on Revolution Square. Building started in 1928 and finished 10 years later. The building survived a big earthquake in 1931, during its construction, but was badly damaged in the 1972 quake. It had to be condemned and closed down as it had become dangerous. However it is still standing and there are hopes to restore it one day.

In 1991, the **Immaculate Conception Cathedral** was opened to replace the Old Cathedral. It's an interesting design that's nicknamed 'La Chichona' because the locals think the cupolas on the roof look like breasts – chiches is slang for breasts.

Another modern building, on Revolution Square, is the **Rubén Darío National Theater.** Named after a famous Nicaraguan poet, it was opened in 1969. It holds fashion shows, concerts and art exhibitions.

MANAGUA
NICARAGUA

'Adios' from Managua, the capital of Nicaragua. 'Adios' might mean 'goodbye' in most other parts of the Spanish-speaking world, but in Nicaragua it is often used as a greeting. Around 1,072,000 live in a city that has experienced more than its fair share of disasters – caused by nature and by people. Situated on Lake Managua, it also has several lagoons within the city.

The **National Palace** is one of the oldest buildings to have survived the 1972 earthquake completely intact. It was built in 1940 and used to be a government building. It is now a 'Palace of Culture' and contains the national library, a museum and an art gallery.

Directly opposite is the **Presidential House**, also known as the **Orange House**. From its opening in 1999, to 2007 it was the home of the President. Since then it has been called the House of the People and is used for ceremonial events.

HISTORY

Managua was made the capital of Nicaragua in 1852. It was chosen as a compromise because the two large rival cities of León and Granada wouldn't agree to let the other become the main city. Managua lies between the two. It is believed that it gets its name either from the Nahuatl word meaning 'near the water', or from the Mangue word meaning 'leader'.

The city lies on geological fault lines and often suffers from earthquakes. Massive quakes in 1938 and 1972 killed thousands of people and destroyed much of the infrastructure leaving many more homeless. The city has also been the focus of revolution and civil war.

MONEY

While you are in Managua you will be spending the Nicaraguan córdoba. It is named after the founder of Nicaragua, Francisco Hernández de Córdoba.

PLACES TO GO

Dennis Martínez National Stadium

Sports lovers should pay a visit to the Dennis Martínez National Stadium – another structure lucky enough to survive the '72 quake. It was built in 1948 and is named after the first Nicaraguan to play Major League Baseball. Baseball is the national sport and obsession, but the stadium is also a venue for football matches and music concerts.

A volcano or two

Managua sits on the banks of Lake Managua, also known as Xolotlán Lake. The area is very volcanic and you can take a trip to the Momotombo volcano – be careful though, as it's still quite active. A little further away is another volcano called Cerro Negro. If you're feeling intrepid you can surf down its volcanic sand!

MANAGUA
NICARAGUA

FOOD

Spotted rooster and tripe soup

The national dish of Nicaragua is undoubtedly *Gallo Pinto*. The name means 'spotted rooster', but vegetarians can enjoy it because it contains no chicken! It's made from rice and beans and it is so named because the colours look like the colours of rooster feathers. It is eaten at any time of day, and often for breakfast.

Those with a stronger stomach might like to try the chewy *Sopa de Mondongo*. It is a soup made from tripe (pig or cow's stomach) and assorted vegetables.

Cornmeal and cacao

You can wash all of this down with a nice glass of *pinolillo*, a traditional drink made from sweetened cornmeal and cacao. You might need to sweeten it further as it is quite bitter on its own.

Sopa de Mondongo

Gallo Pinto

Pinolillo

THINGS TO DO

Tour Tiscapa Lagoon

Lake Managua is very polluted but there are some cleaner lagoons in the city. The most popular is Tiscapa. Here you can take a canopy tour – glide over the trees and lagoon on a high zip wire.

Overseeing everything that happens at the lagoon is a huge statue of Augusto César Sandino (1895–1934). He is the revolutionary figure whose name was adopted by the Sandinista political party who overthrew the government in 1979.

Follow in the footsteps of ancient humans

A short walk from the banks of Lake Managua you will find an archaeological site dedicated to another short walk. About 2,100 years ago a group of around 15 people strolled across some mudflats. Their footprints dried out and were perfectly preserved. The prints were rediscovered in 1874 and are now protected by a museum, which has been built over them. The museum (Museo Arqueológico Huellas de Acahualinca) also contains other ancient artifacts from around the area, including pottery and early tools.

Tiscapa Lagoon

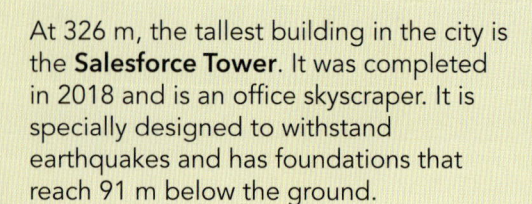

At 326 m, the tallest building in the city is the **Salesforce Tower**. It was completed in 2018 and is an office skyscraper. It is specially designed to withstand earthquakes and has foundations that reach 91 m below the ground.

SF's most iconic building is probably the **Transamerica Pyramid**, completed in 1972. The bottom of the building has a park with redwood trees and a fountain decorated with frog sculptures.

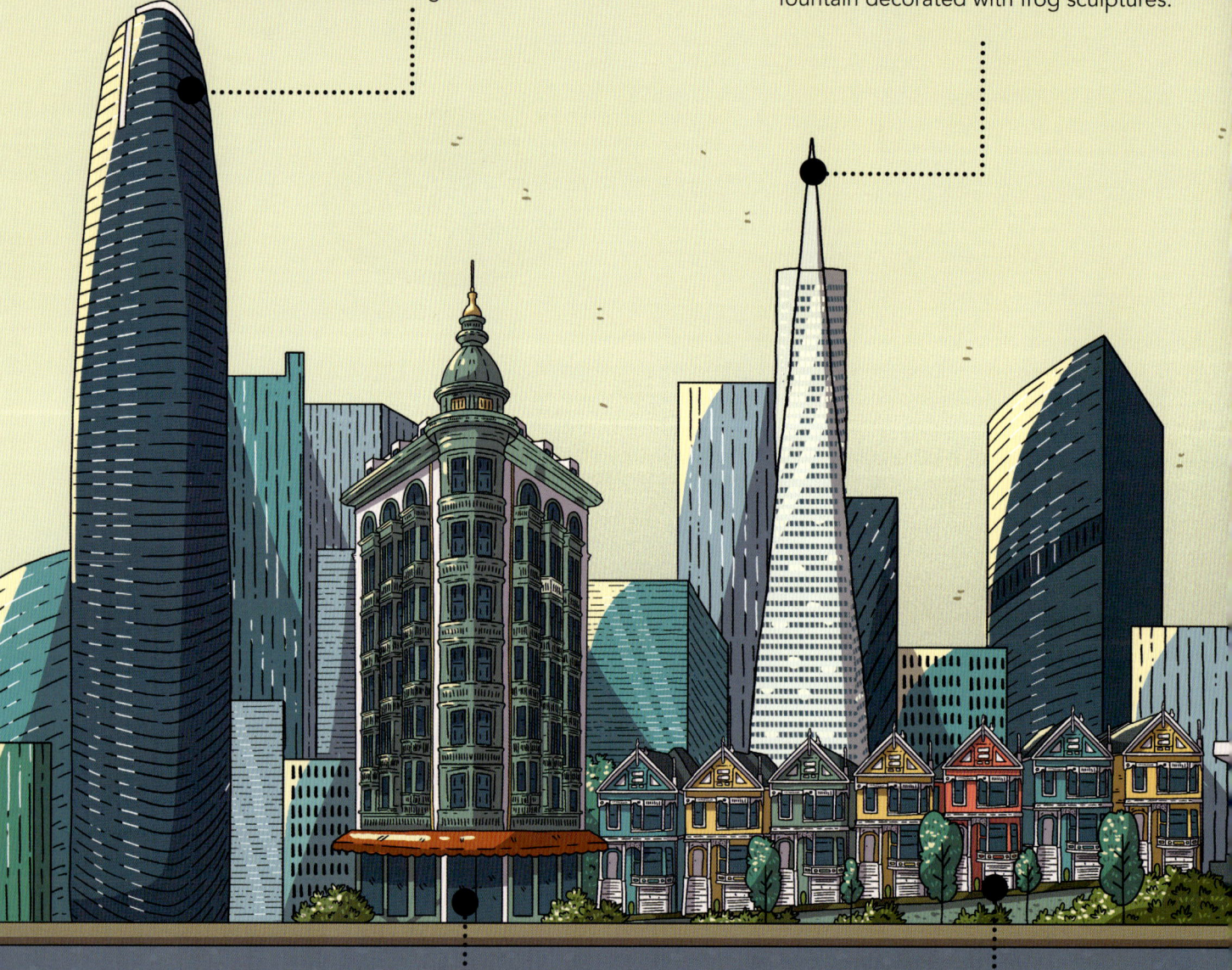

One block down from the Pyramid is another familiar SF landmark, **Columbus Tower**, also known as the Sentinel Building. It was built in 1907 and is now home to a movie studio called American Zoetrope.

The **Painted Ladies** are a group of seven Victorian houses, built in the 1890s. They are often featured in films and TV series set in the city.

SAN FRANCISCO
USA

It's a 'hella' big welcome to San Francisco! 'Hella' is a San Franciscan term meaning 'very'. San Francisco, San Fran, Frisco, SF, or 'The City' as it's known to its 883,305 inhabitants, is the second-most densely populated city in the US after New York. It is situated on a peninsula and therefore you are never far from the sea. Because of the sea and the city's many hills, it has microclimates, so it can be boiling hot inland and pretty chilly in 'The City'. It is also famous for its dense summer fog!

The oldest building in town is the **Mission Dolores**. It was built by the Spanish in 1791 to try to convert the local tribes to Christianity.

The **Cathedral of Saint Mary of the Assumption** was built in 1971 and replaced an eighteenth-century cathedral now known as Old St Mary's Church.

The **de Young Museum** is a fine arts museum in Golden Gate Park. It is constructed in copper and designed so that as the metal oxidises the building will turn green and blend into the surroundings.

39

HISTORY

As its name suggests, San Francisco was originally a Spanish colonial town. It was founded in 1776 and named after St Francis of Assissi. It became Mexican in 1821, but was claimed by the United States in 1848, after the Mexican-American War. The Americans got lucky because that same year gold was discovered in Northern California. The tiny town of around a thousand people became a thriving city of 25,000 in less than a year as people flocked there to make their fortunes.

The city has had some setbacks, however: in 1851, nine people died and three quarters of the city was destroyed by fire. In 1906, a devastating earthquake struck – gas mains burst and fires spread rapidly. Around 80 per cent of the city was destroyed and around 3,000 people killed. In recent years, SF has prospered due to the nearby information technology industry and it has a reputation of being one of the nicest places to live in the USA.

MONEY

Like everyone else in the USA, San Franciscans use US dollars to pay for things. They need a lot of them though as it is one of the most expensive places to live in the USA.

Lombard Street

PLACES TO GO

Famous Streets

There are so many places to go in San Francisco that it's difficult to choose! Take a walk down Lombard Street. It may take longer than you think and you may get a little dizzy as you negotiate its twists and turns.

Fisherman's Wharf

After the dizziness has passed make your way to Fisherman's Wharf and enjoy browsing the tourist shops and sampling the sea. You can watch the seals sunbathing on Pier 39 as you wait for a ferry to take you to Alcatraz.

Alcatraz

Until 1963, Alcatraz was a prison located on an island in San Francisco Bay. It was home to notorious prisoners including the gangsters Al Capone and 'Machine Gun' Kelly. In 1973, ten years after the last prisoner left, it was opened to the public, as part of the Golden Gate National Recreation Centre. Be wary if you visit though – it's supposed to be haunted!

Alcatraz

SAN FRANCISCO
USA

FOOD

Fish stew SF style

Cioppino, the defining dish of SF, was invented there. It's a delicious fish stew invented by Italian fishermen in the city. Legend has it that the fishermen would all 'chip in' a bit of their catch to make a meal. The seafood mixture, usually crab, shrimp, clams and fish, was added to onions, herbs, garlic and tomatoes to make a delicious meal.

Burrito city

The other signature dish of San Fran is the 'mission burrito'. It gets its name from the Mission area of the city and is bigger than ordinary burritos because the tortillas are steamed, stretched and filled with extra rice, beans and the filling of your choice.

Mission burrito

Cioppino

Golden Gate Bridge

THINGS TO DO

Gaze at the Golden Gate Bridge

The Golden Gate Bridge is one of the most famous landmarks in the world and well worth a view. Some of the best views of the bridge are from The Presidio, a former military base, but now a park filled with trees and flowers.

Take a trip

You cannot visit Frisco without taking a trip on one of the famous cable cars, but they can get very crowded. If the queues are too long, you could always hop on one of the (slightly more modern) streetcars.

Cable car

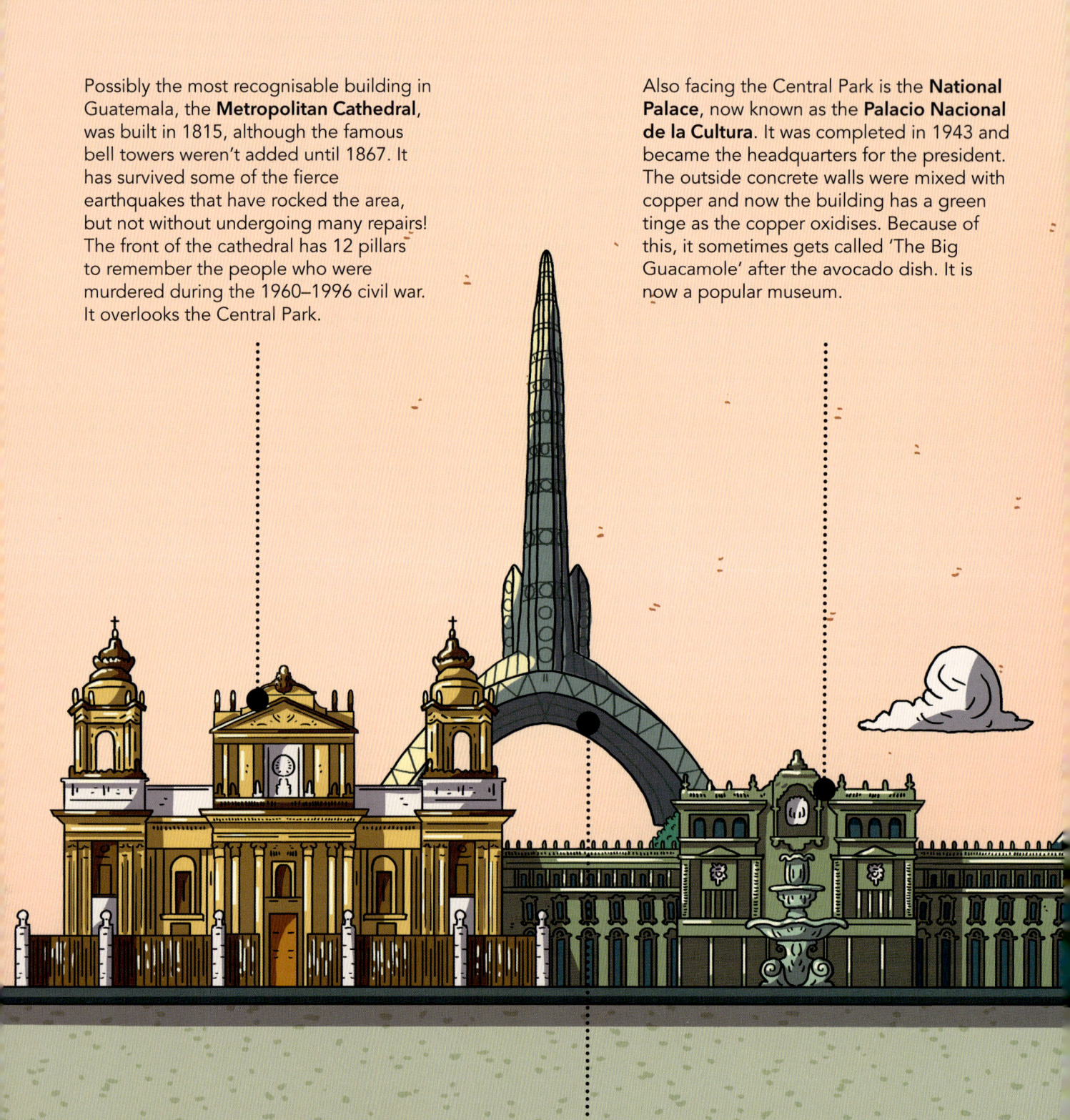

Possibly the most recognisable building in Guatemala, the **Metropolitan Cathedral**, was built in 1815, although the famous bell towers weren't added until 1867. It has survived some of the fierce earthquakes that have rocked the area, but not without undergoing many repairs! The front of the cathedral has 12 pillars to remember the people who were murdered during the 1960–1996 civil war. It overlooks the Central Park.

Also facing the Central Park is the **National Palace**, now known as the **Palacio Nacional de la Cultura**. It was completed in 1943 and became the headquarters for the president. The outside concrete walls were mixed with copper and now the building has a green tinge as the copper oxidises. Because of this, it sometimes gets called 'The Big Guacamole' after the avocado dish. It is now a popular museum.

The **Tower of the Reformer** was built in 1935 to celebrate 100 years since the birth of Justo Rufino Barrios, a former president who made important changes to the country in the nineteenth century.

GUATEMALA CITY
GUATEMALA

Guatemalans are known for their politeness and formality and consider 'Hola' to be a bit too casual a greeting... so, depending on what time of day it is, it's 'buenos dias' (good morning), 'buenas tardes' (good afternoon), or 'buenas noches' (good evening) to Guatemala City. Its full name is New Guatemala of the Assumption. Around 2.5 million people live in the cultural and financial centre of the country of Guatemala.

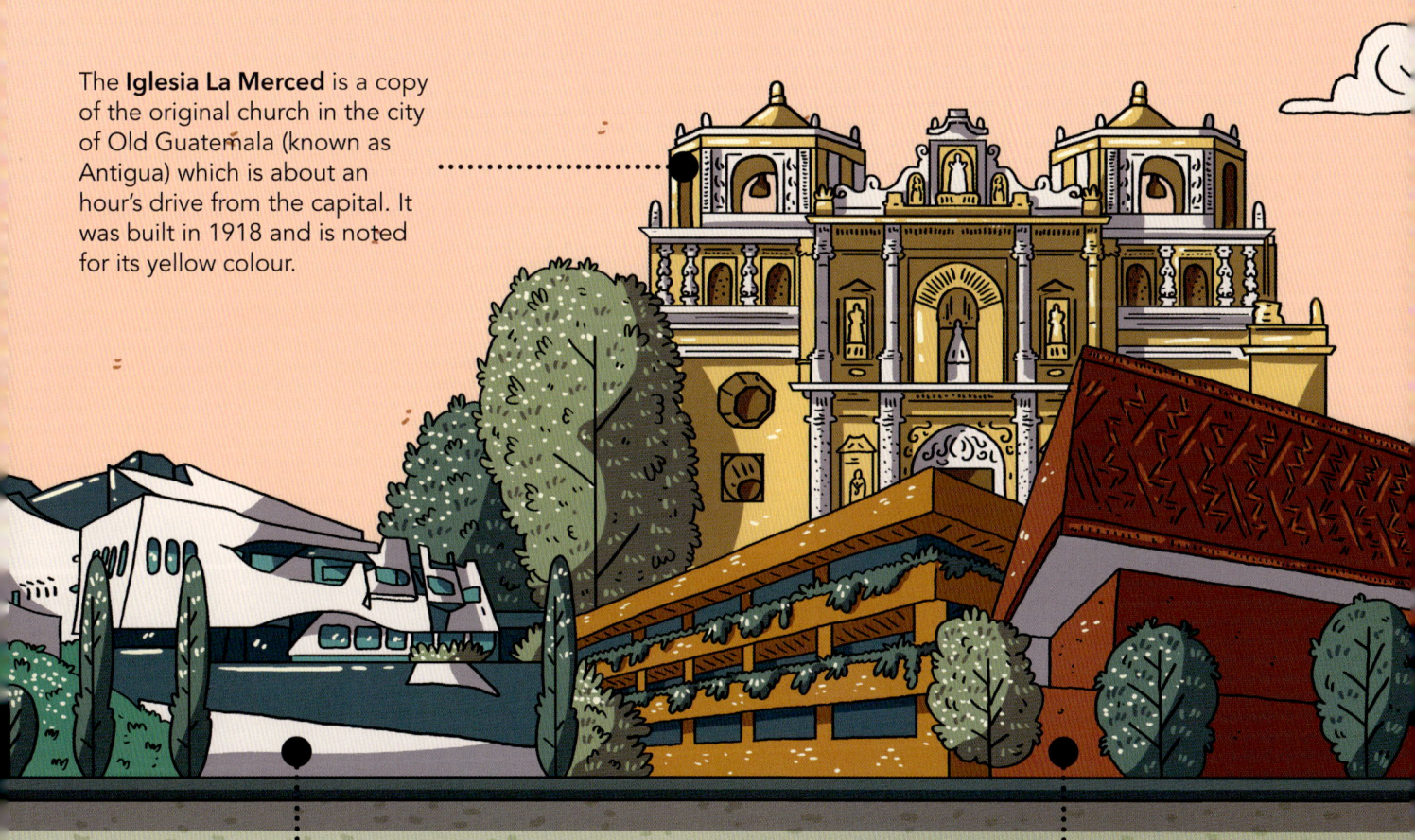

The **Iglesia La Merced** is a copy of the original church in the city of Old Guatemala (known as Antigua) which is about an hour's drive from the capital. It was built in 1918 and is noted for its yellow colour.

The **Guatemalan National Theater and Miguel Ángel Asturias Cultural Centre** was originally built as a military fortress. It is named after a famous Guatemalan Nobel-Prize-winning writer. The design is supposed to represent a jaguar resting with its paw out.

Two beautiful, modern museums, the **Popol Vuh Museum** and the **Ixchel Museum of Indigenous Textiles and Clothing** are next to each other on the university campus. Both house a wealth of artefacts from the ancient Mayan culture of the area. Ixchel is the Mayan jaguar goddess of the Moon.

HISTORY

The name 'Guatemala' originates from a word meaning 'place of many trees'. The country has had an unstable history because of its geography. It is in a volcanic area and has suffered many big earthquakes. Its economy used to be based largely on fruit production and was controlled by companies in the USA. This led to economic inequality, which in turn led to much violence and civil war. Guatemala City, which became the capital in 1847, now has a much more balanced and robust economy.

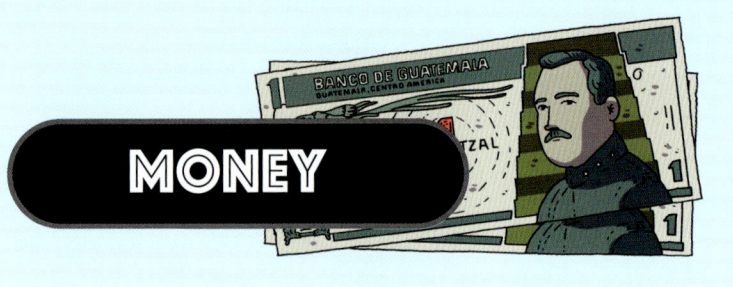

MONEY

Guatemala must be the only country to officially name their currency after its national bird, the quetzal! The ancient Mayans in the area used to use the tail feathers of the quetzal bird as currency.

PLACES TO GO

Antigua

About an hour's drive from the capital is Old Guatemala, also known as Antigua. The architecture here is so beautiful that it has been designated a world heritage site. Many buildings in Antigua inspired the architecture of the capital. The original yellow La Merced Church is here, as well as the famous seventeenth-century Santa Catalina Arch. The arch was the inspiration for the post office building in Guatemala City.

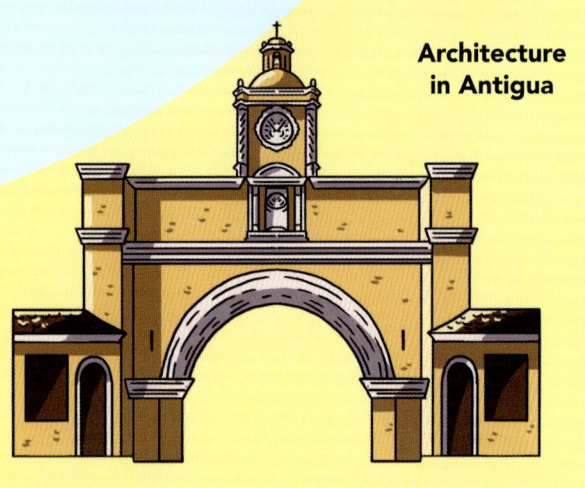

Architecture in Antigua

GUATEMALA CITY
GUATEMALA

FOOD

Home of chocolate

Guatemala claims to be the place that chocolate was invented and you will find plenty of shops making and selling all things chocolaty.

Pepián

The national dish of Guatemala is *Pepián*. It's a thick, meaty stew with vegetables and spicy peppers. The sauce is thickened by adding seeds and nuts.

Roasted ants

If you are feeling more adventurous (and you are visiting in May) you may care to try *Zompopos de Mayo*. This is a seasonal dish only eaten in May and consists of roasted leaf-cutter ants. They have a peanutty taste and are considered to be a delicacy. Delicious!

Chocolate

Pepián

Roasted ants

THINGS TO DO

See the Relief Map of Guatemala

You have a chance to see the whole of Guatemala just by visiting the Relief Map of Guatemala, situated in the north of the city. It is an incredibly detailed 1:10,000 scale map showing the cities and countryside of the entire country. It was constructed in 1905 by the engineer Francisco Vela. He even included an underground tank to supply the 'rivers'!

Relief Map of Guatemala

MORE NORTH AMERICAN CITIES

OTTAWA, CANADA

Ottawa, the capital city of Canada, is named after the river that runs through it. Every winter, it has the world's biggest naturally occurring skating rink when part of the Rideau Canal freezes over.

Population: 1,407,928 (2021)

Highest building: Claridge Tower (143 m)

Places to see: Rideau Canal, Parliament Hill, National Gallery of Canada

SAN JUAN, PUERTO RICO

San Juan was founded by the Spanish in 1519. It's the capital of Puerto Rico, which is a territory of the USA. Originally, Columbus called the island San Juan and the city was called Puerto Rico – over time they swapped names!

Population: 323,279 (2021)

Highest building: Coliseum Tower Residences (78.88 m)

Places to see: Fort San Felipe del Morro, Fort San Cristóbal, La Fortaleza

KINGSTON, JAMAICA

Kingston is the capital city and biggest port in Jamaica. It was founded in 1692 after an earthquake destroyed the nearby town of Port Royal. There is a contrast in the city between the modern buildings and the older ones that have survived the hurricanes and earthquakes. One of the most beautiful older buildings is Devon House, built in 1881 and now a museum.

Population: 592,000 (2021)

Highest building: Jamaica Pegasus Hotel (61 m)

Places to see: Devon House, Bob Marley Museum, Giddy House

CALGARY, CANADA

Calgary has been ranked as one of the best places to live on the planet. It is one of the cleanest cities on Earth and has very heavy fines for littering. It is famous for the Calgary Stampede, which happens in July each year. It claims to be the largest outdoor show on earth. Thousands of people come to watch rodeos and exhibitions. The event started in 1886 and has earned the city the nicknames 'Cowtown' and 'Stampede City'.

Population: 1,518,000 (2021)

Highest building: Brookfield Place (247 m)

Places to see: National Music Centre, Heritage Park Historical Village, Calgary Stampede

LAS VEGAS, USA

Las Vegas is Spanish for 'the meadows' and couldn't be more inappropriate for this desert city. It was a tiny town until the area legalised gambling in 1931. Since then, its economy has rapidly grown as millions of tourists flock to gamble and enjoy the exciting nightlife. Its reputation has earned it the nickname 'Sin City'.

Population: 2,772,000 (2021)

Highest building: Stratosphere Tower (350 m)

Places to see: The fountains at Bellagio, The gondolas at The Venetian, Luxor Hotel

CHICAGO, USA

Chicago, on Lake Michigan, is known as 'The Windy City' and while it can be blustery, most people think the nickname comes from the 'hot air' that come from its noisy politicians. The city is famous for notorious gangsters like Al Capone, and its deep-pan pizza. It's the third-biggest city in the USA after New York and Los Angeles.

Population: 2,679,080 (2021)

Highest building: Willis Tower (442 m)

Places to see: Cloud Gate ('The Bean'), Navy Pier, Art Institute of Chicago

PORT-AU-PRINCE, HAITI

Port-Au-Prince became the capital of French-ruled Haiti in 1770. It was burned down in 1791 when the slaves on the island fought and took control of the island from the people that enslaved them. Its main exports today are the same as they were back then: coffee and sugar.

Population: 2,843,925

Highest building: Gala Tower/Digicel Building (joint at 47 m)

Places to see: Cathedral of Our Lady of the Assumption (this was destroyed by an earthquake in 2010 but there are plans to rebuild it), National Museum of Haiti, Maison Dufort

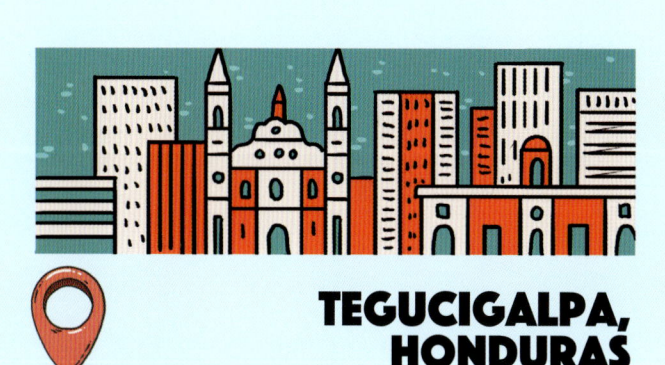

TEGUCIGALPA, HONDURAS

Tegucigalpa means 'Hills of Silver' and the capital is famous for its silver mines. Its long name is often shortened to 'Tegus'. It was very badly damaged by Hurricane Mitch in 1998 when mudslides destroyed homes and killed many people. The devastation was so great that it was decided never to use the name 'Mitch' for a hurricane ever again.

Population: 1,485,300

Highest building: Vitri Tower (116 m)

Places to see: Museum for National Identity, Church of Santa María de los Dolores, San Miguel Cathedral, Central Park, Basilica of the Virgin of Suyapa

GLOSSARY

Art Deco
a decorative style of art and architecture dating from the 1920s and 1930s.

autonomous territory
a part of a nation that has some independent control over how it is governed.

Aztec culture
a Mexican indigenous culture that thrived from 1300 to 1521.

civil war
a war between people from the same country.

colonised
to settle in and rule over someone else's country.

constitutional monarchy
when a king or queen has power but it is limited by the law.

cupola
a rounded dome on a roof.

downtown
an American English term usually relating to the main cultural or business part of a town or city.

Indigenous people
the original or earliest known people in an area.

infrastructure
the buildings, structures and facilities that are needed for a society to function.

Mangue
an extinct Central American language.

Maya Empire
a civilisation that thrived in Central America from 1800 BCE to 900 CE.

metropolitan area
the densely populated centre of a city and its less-populated surrounding towns and neighbourhoods that still fall within its boundaries.

microclimate
a localised set of climate conditions that are different from those nearby.

Nahuatl
the language of the Aztecs, which is still spoken in Mexico today.

Sandinistas
a socialist political party in Nicaragua.

socialism
a political movement that tries to share resources more equally amongst the population.

INDEX

Alaska 5
Calgary 4, 46
Canada 5, 10–13, 22–25, 46
Chicago 47
Cuba 18–21
Greenland 26–29
Guatemala 42–45
Guatemala City 42–45
Haiti 47
Havana 18–21
Honduras 47
Iqaluit 5
Jamaica 46
Kingston 4, 46
Las Vegas 4, 47
Managua 4, 34–37
Mexico 6–9
Mexico City 4, 6–9
Montreal 4, 22–25
New York 4, 14–17
Nicaragua 34–37
Nuuk 4, 26–29
Ottawa 4, 46
Port–au–Prince 4, 47
Puerto Rico 46
San Francisco 4, 38–41
San Juan 4, 46
Tegucigalpa 4, 47
Toronto 4, 10–13
USA 14–17, 30–33, 38–41, 47
Washington, D.C. 4, 30–33

48